This non-fictional story is my only hope of proving my innocence, so this cannot possibly fail. Please, I'm begging you, tell the world about this injustice caused by my wife's lies. If they catch me, I'll be falsely prosecuted for domestic abuse. And no good lawyer will defend me, because every last dollar of my savings went towards the production of this story. Oh and, if you happen to see my wife or anyone I've ever known, they'll try lying to you by saying that drawing of me is fake. Don't listen to them, this is 100% what I look like in real life.

Copyright © 2025 Sagan P. Gabos

All rights reserved.

No part of this publication may be reproduced, distributed, or transmitted in any form or by any means, including photocopying, recording, or other electronic or mechanical methods, without the prior written permission of the publisher, except as permitted by U.S. copyright law. For permission requests, or any questions, contact

"sayagainsagan@gmail.com"

The story, all names, characters, and incidents portrayed in this production are fictitious. No identification with actual persons (living or deceased), places, buildings, and products is intended or should be inferred.

Index

Chapter	Page
1	7
2	15
3	29
4	39
5	51
6	55
7	75
8	83

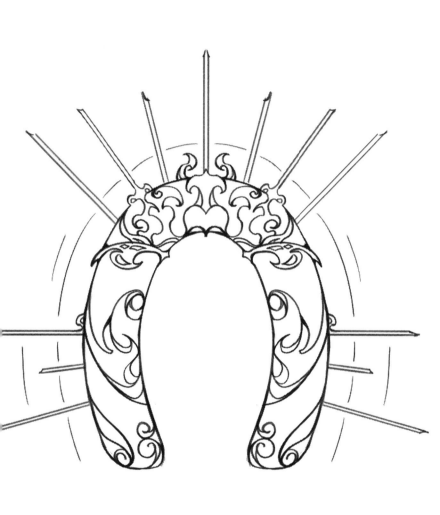

Le First Chapter

William's Life Changing Decision

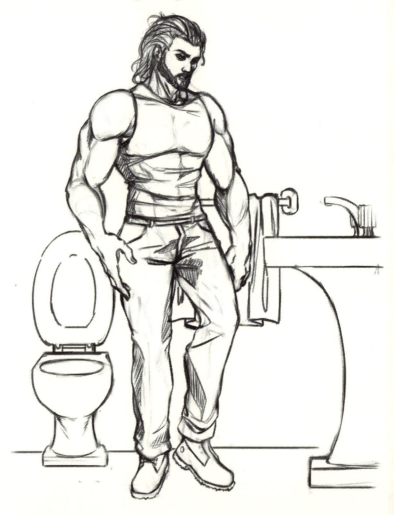

Another night, yet another two-liter of Toilet Dew™ effortlessly chugged by the small town of Grand Bowl's local lumberjack, William Wangle.

"*Buuuuuuuuuurp* Another one down boys!" William bragged into his gaming headset.

That had been the third liter he had downed in his two hours of playing his favorite game, **"Call of Pooty™, Toilet Warfare"**. Such a grand feat brought much joy to his fellow online gamer bros.

"Hell yeah, Willy Willy Wangle! You're gonna break your record in no time at this rate!" His friend Nathan cheered on.

"Chug a fourth! Chug a fourth!" Another friend named Edward chanted.

"TOILET!" His religious toilet-fanatic friend Fernando rejoiced at the top of his lungs.

As William began opening up his fourth bottle, Mother Nature called for him. "Speaking of toilets, I need to go use mine."

He threw his headset off, stood up from his Sitter Shitter Gaming Chair™, and rushed to the Toiletroom. It was only while moving that he realized how full his bladder was.

Once William made it to his Toiletroom, he went down on his knees to perform the **'Prayer of Grateful Waste'**. Despite how badly he had to pee, he knew it was a sin to not perform the prayer before using a toilet.

"Oh great toilet of mine, may you take the waste I offer you. Whether it be pee or poo, may the 1.6 to 7 gallons of water you use to take it away, and..."

An invasive thought suddenly brought William's prayer to an end. One that had never crossed his mind before that very moment.

"Wait, why would I waste so much water just to pee?"

After pondering this for a moment or two, William stood back up with a new sense of curiosity. And after another moment of pondering, his eyes would lock onto the Toiletroom's complementary sink.

"Wouldn't pissing in the sink use much less?"

William undid his pants, turned the faucet on, and began to relive himself in the sink. He couldn't help but feel guilty as he watched his pee go down the sink's drain.

Not only was he performing an unspeakable sin by not using the toilet, but willingly leaving the sacred prayer unfinished was straight-up blasphemy.

…However, William couldn't deny this method was using significantly less water than if he had relieved himself in the toilet. So much less in fact, that he began to wonder why peeing in the toilet was required by law and his religion. He wouldn't have long to think on this though, as-

"OH MY TOILET!!! WHAT ARE YOU DOING?!" William's wife cried out while looking in the bathroom, due to him forgetting to close the door.

"**gasp** S-Sweety, I can explain! I was only-"

William turned to her and accidentally peed on her dress. While her skin was pale from the terror of

what she was witnessing, her face gave away just how enraged and disgusted she was. Never before had he seen his wife stare at him with such a horrific mix of emotions.

"I-I'm so sorry! I didn't mean to-"

"Y-You no good dirty Sink Pisser!!!"

His wife stormed off while visibly shaking with rage. And while William knew there was no chance of calming his justifiably enraged wife down, that wouldn't stop him from following after her to at least try.

"I swear, it was just this one time!" He grabbed her by the arm. "This isn't a normal-"

She turned around and smacked him in the face.

"I can't believe I've been married to a Sink Pisser all this time!" She kneed him in the nuts, as tears rolled down her eyes. "Our relationship was nothing more than a sick twisted lie!!!"

//

She stormed out of their house, slamming the front door behind her. The force of the slam knocked many framed photos, toilet merchandise, and toilet-related religious symbols off the hallway walls. Most of these shattered or broke all around William as they made contact with the floor.

While slowly recovering, William's eyes fixated on one particular photo. It was of him and his wife sitting on the first toilet they had ever bought together.

Thinking back on that moment of true love brought a warm smile to his face. The nostalgic joy was woefully short-lived, as the reality of his situation fully sank in.

"Sweety, I'm so sorry!!!" He cried out at the top of his lungs while bawling his eyes out.

William's crying was so intense that he took a full minute to stand up. Though to him, this 'minute' felt like an agonizing hour. Time truly meant nothing to a man whose world had been destroyed by his own hands.

Once finally up, he made his way back over to the Sitter Shitter Gaming Chair™. After downing another liter of Toilet Dew™ to regain his composure, William put his headset back on to let the gamer bros know what happened.

"Guys, I messed up bad! I messed up really bad!" He confessed to his friends.

"You're damn right, you no good Sink Pisser!!!" Nathan shouted, sounding nearly unhinged with rage.

The horrible realization hit William harder than his wife kneeing him in the nuts. "You guys heard all that?!"

"Yep! We heard everything!" Edward yelled. **"How could you throw away your marriage like that?!"**

"Gu-Guys, please! Let me-"

"TOILET!!!" Fernando the religious toilet fanatic roared while smashing sounds could be heard in

the background.

"TOOOOILEEEEEEEET!!!!!!!!!"

William was then kicked from the game lobby. Immediately after, he received a message from Big Toilet informing him that his online account was banned for life. Finally, just to add insult to injury, he received another message telling him that his electricity would be cut off… Which immediately happened when he finished reading said message.

All he could do was sit silently in the darkness, while blankly staring forward. A part of him hoped and prayed that it was all just a bad dream. Eventually, though, he had to accept that his life was ruined.

"What have I done?!" William cried out while breaking down in tears. "I never should have **peed in the sink!!!**"

Le Second Chapter

William's Talk With A Righteous Reaper

Once the realization that his life was ruined beyond repair set in, William knew he was going to need something more than just Toilet Dew™ alone to cheer him up. So he spent the next few hours in his dim candle-lit kitchen brewing up something very special… Toilet Shine.

"Alright, what's the next step?" He asked himself while looking over a list of instructions written on a dirty piece of paper.

The "Recipe" William used was his own creation he had come up with one drunken night during a house party. The party in question was to celebrate the brand-new battery-powered Pooer Brewer™ that he and his wife had purchased.

Said recipe read as follows…

Recapy for Toilet Dew Recipy

1: Pour 2 Gallans of Toilet Water Brand Vodka in Pooer Brewer.

2: Powur 7 Littters of Toilet Dewin.   also por cup for self,

3:

4: taste test mixture, add more Vodka or Dew ass neaded or want.

3: Set Pooer Brewer two low or medium or high mixing.

4: Taste tet Mixtur then ad Vodka and Dew a neded or needed or needed or wanted.

5: Don't get drunk while test testing and pee in wrong toilet. Makes Toilet Shine taste bad.

6:

After carefully reading it over, William smiled while happily lifting a soup ladle worth of the shine to his face.

"Looks like it's time for the second taste test."

With a sniff of his nose and a lick of his lips, William was ready to take himself to Drunks R Us™. Just as it was about to touch his lips though, his phone went off. His eyes lit up with hope as he dropped the ladle in reckless joy, accidentally covering the floor in sticky alcohol.

"That must be her!"

William quickly pulled his phone out and nearly dropped it in his excitement. He could barely contain himself and answered it without bothering to check the caller ID.

"Honey, I'm so glad you called! I was getting worried that-"

"I am *not* your 'Honey', Mr. Wangle." The deep and cold voice of an older-sounding man interrupted. "She should be the last thing on your mind right now."

The desperate hope William had been clinging onto for hours was utterly decimated in the blank of an eye. There was no time for sadness though, as he was more confused than anything else.

"Who is this? W-What are you talking about?"

"You know **what** I'm talking about… *Sink Pisser.*"

A frost-burningly cold shiver went down William's spine. "How did you-"

"And as for **who** you're talking to.." The man interrupted. "I am a high-ranking member of the Toilet-Quisition."

"T-T-Toilet-Quisition?!"

William had heard many stories and legends of the Toilet-Quisition. So many in fact, that he assumed they were nothing more than a conspiracy theory… But now, he had been proven wrong in the worst way imaginable.

"Please, Mr. Toilet-Quisitor Sir!" William begged, not bothering to hide the uncut and unprocessed fear in his voice. "You have to believe me! I've dedicated my life to-"

"**Shut it.**" The Toilet-Quisitor silenced. "**You** have been found guilty by not only the Grand Toilet-Quisition but also Big Toilet's Board of Directors and the Supreme Toilet Court. No amount of excuses will convince me or anyone else of your 'innocence'."

Didn't take long for William to realize his life wasn't just ruined, but the entire world that he was taught from birth to worship had turned on him. He was now nothing more than a blasphemous **Sink Pisser** in the eyes of the powers that be. Despite all the horrifying thoughts and fears that went through his mind, there was only one question he could think to ask at that moment.

"Why did you call if you weren't willing to hear me out?"

"To warn you."

"...Warn me?"

"Yes, Mr. Wangle. You see-"

"Excuse me, Sir?" A woman, who sounded to be around 18, was heard interrupting the Toilet-Quisitor. "The driver wanted me to inform you that he's ready."

The Toilet-Quisitor let out a low and hateful grunt before going completely silent. William could feel the uncomfortable tension through his phone, preparing for the man to go off on the poor woman... Instead, he was surprised to hear a calm reply.

"Oh, you're the new girl I assume?"

"Ye- Yes sir. I started last week." The woman replied, sounding a little nervous.

"...Listen, just so you know, *NEVER* interrupt a Toilet-Quisitor in the middle of a call.." He calmly explained, while clearly holding back anger.

"*gulp* I'm sorry sir, I won't do it again."

"You'd be wise not to, as others won't be as forgiving... Now, go tell the driver I'm in the middle of an important call and will be ready to go when I'm done."

"Yes sir, and thank you for letting me off easy for my-"

"Leave me to my business..."

"S-Sorry Sir."

The woman was heard speed walking away, without saying another word. The Toilet-Quisitor sighed.

"Now where were we? Oh right... You see, Mr. Wangle, your betrayal of all toilet-kind can not go unpunished. However, that punishment must be carried out publicly, and by one such as I. Or else, said punishment will go unnoticed by the public at large."

It didn't take long for William to fully grasp what was in store for him. "Y-You're going to publicly execute me?!"

"Yes, Mr. Wangle. Extreme examples must be made of all who go against the status quo. You should have known something like this would happen when you chose to piss in that sink."

"But I was just curious! I swear I'll never-!"

"You know what they say about curiosity, *right?*" The Toilet-Quisitor interrupted, clearly tired of listening to his pleas. "I'm about to head down there right now. You better not get yourself killed before I can properly put you down myself. Organizing these types of things already requires a lot of time and taxpayer money, and I'd rather not have all that go to waste."

William assumed this was just a fancy way of saying "don't kill yourself". However, after thinking over the wording a bit more, he second-guessed himself.

"What's that supposed to mean?!"

The Toilet-Quisitor let out an impatient sigh. "Mr. Wangle, according to this intel I've gathered, your wife's father is well known in your small town for serving as a 'Big Toilet Licenced Bounty Hunter' in his prime years, till retiring to be a Toilet Preacher. Now tell me, do you think a man like that is going to sit by and let a Sink Pissing Sinner like you go unpunished?"

William had forgotten entirely about The Father, as the two were never close. Hell, the last time the two ever talked was when they happened to run into one another at their local grocery store. Even then, it was just awkward small talk. However, now that the old bounty hunter had been forcibly brought to the forefront of his mind, he could only shudder in silence.

"Can I assume by your silence that you understand the danger you're in?"

"..."

"Good, now keep yourself alive until I can arrive to properly end your life. Sounds simple, correct?"

The Toilet-Quisitor immediately hung up, giving William no chance to respond. Though it was likely he would have remained silent even if given the chance, as his mind had been entangled in a conflicting web of despair and dread.

A part of him attempted to brainstorm ways to leave town and potentially escape his fate. However, the other more hopeless part of him wondered if he'd rather be murdered by his wife's father, or killed publicly by the Toilet-Quisitor. Before this inner conflict could really go anywhere, William was abruptly pulled into reality by-

SHATTER

"Ahhh! Holy Toilet, what in the Sink Pissing Hell was that!?" William cried out, as one of his living room windows was shattered.

He grabbed a candle and rushed into his living room to investigate. Carefully looking around to avoid any broken glass, William eventually discovered it was the window closest to the stairs that had been vandalized. After approaching the newly made opening to look out and see who was responsible, he was met with a truly terrifying sight.

Outside stood The Father, and four younger-looking men, all dressed in low-ranked Big Toilet Bounty Hunter outfits, and armed with bean bag shotguns. William's wife was also seen standing next to her father with a look of pure hate on her face. However, that was nothing compared to the nearly unhinged rage that was visibly displayed by her father.

"Sink Pisser!" Her father boomed in his preacher-like voice while shaking from his barely contained rage. "Not only have you turned your back on your faith, but you have also betrayed my daughter's trust! Men like you deserve nothing more than a bullet to the brain and a cold dark grave! Now, step out and face your fate like a man, or we will drag you out here like an animal and force you to face it!"

William knew he would never be able to talk things over with a man like him. If anything, trying to talk to him would likely have made things **significantly** worse. So instead, William decided the best course of action was to lock the front and back doors and barricade them with anything he could find. But despite the effort being put into this, he ultimately knew how doomed he was.

"I'm so screwed! I'm so fucking screwed!!! How the fuck am I going to get myself out of this?!"

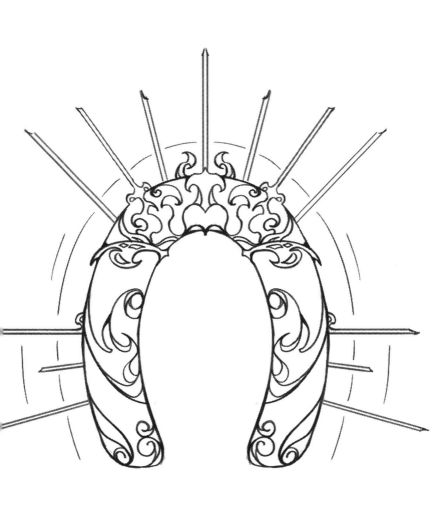

Le Third Chapter

The Unrelenting Rage Of A Fanatical Father

A few minutes passed, and The Father's barely-held-together patience ran thin. The four men began to wonder why he didn't just order them to rush in and grab William. They lacked the courage to ask him directly though, so instead one of them, a bounty hunter in training named Noah, decided to suggest the idea to his daughter.

"Hey, Vanessa?" Noah began whispering. "Can I ask you something?"

"What is it?" She whispered in response, a bit annoyed.

"I don't think your husband-"

"You mean ex-husband?" She sternly corrected, clearly offended.

"Y-yeah, sorry about that."

"Don't **ever** suggest I'd still consider that Sink Pisser to be husband-worthy." She calmed herself down, holding back the urge to yell. "What were you going to say about him?"

Noah carefully thought over his words before speaking. "I uh, I don't think William's gonna come out. We should just go in there and get him."

"...I know, but Big Toilet has strict rules when it comes to engaging heretics, and my Dad is a very 'by-the-books' type of guy."

Noah was about to accept this, until realizing something. "But, he isn't licensed anymore. Plus, we're are just in training, and technically not licensed either."

Vanessa opened her mouth to argue this but immediately realized how good of a point he had made. Without saying another word, she approached her father to get his attention.

"Dad, he doesn't have the balls to come out here on his own. Let's stop wasting our time and just grab him already."

The Father slowly turned to face his daughter. He was glad he chose to wear his blackout glasses that night so she couldn't see the disappointment and slight anger in his eyes.

"Have you forgotten 'The Code Of The Patient Toilet'? I spent many years ensuring you knew everything there is to know. Please don't tell me those years were wasted."

"No Dad, I didn't forget. You're the one who forgot."

"...And what exactly did I forget?"

"That you're retired, and no longer legally obligated to follow that 'Toilet Code'."

The Father stood in complete silence at his daughter. While his face appeared blank and emotionless, the gears in his old mind were beginning to turn.

"By Toilet, you're right!" He turned around to face his men in training, who in response all went into soldier-like stances. "Men, it is clear that William prefers to hide like a coward in the dark. So he must be dragged out here to face the light!"

The men all cheered, excited and ready for action. As all except for one of them stepped forward though-

"Stand your ground!" The Father ordered, in his imposing Preacher voice.

The young men went back into soldier stances. Their short moment of hype was gone and replaced with blind obedience.

"Only two of you will be going in there!" He grabbed the one who didn't step forward. "And you will be the one leading!"

The young man went pale in the face. "Wh- Wh- Wh- What?! Bu-But why me?!"

"Don't play dumb, Jonathan. You are by far the most cowardly one here. Don't think I haven't noticed you always hiding in the back of the group during our manhunts."

The Father shoved the young man towards the house, then turned to face the other men. He looked each of them over for a moment, before pointing at the largest and chubbiest member of the group.

"And you, Matthew, will accompany him."

Matthew appeared a bit surprised at first but began making his way toward Jonathan after only a few moments, with a cocky smile on his face. "You made the right choice choosing me. I'll make sure he doesn't-"

As he was passing by, The Father aggressively pulled him in close. "Don't fuck this up. If *anything* goes wrong in there, you're the one that will suffer the consequences. Am I making myself clear?"

Matthew slowly nodded his head, unable to hide his fear from The Father.

"Very good." The Father shoved him towards Jonathan. "Now go in there and bring that piece of shit out alive!"

Matthew took a moment to regain his footing before he and Jonathan saluted. "We shall not fail you!"

As the two began exaggeratedly marching up to the house, Vanessa watched on in confusion.

"Hey, Dad?" She began whispering. "Why do your trainees all act like they're in the military?"

He thought on this for a moment. "No idea. They just started acting this way one day. I respect their discipline though, so never saw a reason to stop them."

"...Fair enough I guess."

She looked back and watched as Matthew slammed himself against the door in an attempt to bust it open. Jonathan was standing off to the side, looking into the house through the window they shattered.

"Why don't we just go through this window? It's already partially broken, so-"

slam "Let's try-" *slam* "This a few more times!" *slam* "I don't wanna risk one of us getting-" *slam* "Cut by the glass!" *slam*

While watching on, another trainee in the group, named Tyler, approached The Father. "Sir, are you sure you don't want us to help them?"

"This is the only way they will learn." The Father replied, not taking his eyes off the two.
Tyler knew it was wise not to question The Father and simply went back to watching Matthew slam himself against the door.

Inside the house, William was frantically searching through the messy closet in his bedroom. He attempted to remain calm but the aggressive slamming only reminded him of the danger that was forcing its way in.

"Where is it?! Where in the Sink Pissing Hell is it?! I can't face them empty-handed!!" He cried out while tearing the inside of his closet apart.

Despite covering the entirety of the bedroom with clothing and other random junk, William had seemingly made no progress in finding his means of self-defense. But just as he was ready to give up, his knee knocked into something hard laying under a years-old Toilet Dew™ tapestry that was never hung up.

"Oww! Son of a bitch!!"

He flew into a blind rage and threw the tapestry off. Before his rage could escalate any further, he noticed a wooden baseball bat. Not just any wooden baseball bat though.

"By Toilet, I found it…" He slowly lifted the bat out of his closet, bringing it near a candle to get a better look. "I found my old lynching bat!!!"

As William triumphally looked over his bat, childhood memories came flooding back. From the times when he and his father would help his neighbors bludgeon blasphemers to death, or when he joined in on organized attacks against local porta-potty companies after the government made all non-toilet forms of waste disposal illegal.

William's nostalgic joy slowly faded though, as he realized his bat wasn't going to be used for any righteous justice like it used to be. If anything, it was now his only means of defense against such justice he would have normally been so eager to partake in. He wouldn't spend too much time thinking on this, as it suddenly dawned on him that the slamming sounds had came to a stop.

William silently stood in his room, waiting for something to happen. As he did, his mind began thinking up every possible way of entry they could use. These thoughts ranged from normal things like window entry, until quickly escalating to cutting a hole through a roof and even blowing the front door open. Before his mind could delve any further into paranoia though-

SHATTER

He was dragged back to reality by the sounds of more glass breaking. William wasn't sure what window it was, or if they had simply finished breaking through the already broken window, but knew shit was about to get real.

"***deep breath*** Alright William, this is it." He began motivating himself while looking at his bat. "Time to go out there, kick their asses, and… and…"

William's legs and arms began to shake. The short burst of confidence he built up had vanished, as he realized how suicidal his plan sounded out loud.

"What the hell am I thinking?! I'm gonna die if I go out there!"

Now, once again, scared for his life, William silently cowered in his room. All he could think to do was hold his bat up while staring at the room's entrance. If he couldn't work up the guts to go on the offensive, then he could at least stay on the defensive.

Into The Heart
Of A Sink Pisser's House

Back out in the living room, Jonathan had successfully gained entry and was now helping Matthew get inside. Well, "help" as in trying to pull him through the broken window.

"Holy shit man! You need to lose some weight!" Jonathan yelled while pulling with all his strength.

"Or, maybe you need to gain some muscle, little boy!" Matthew retorted, as his chubby belly struggled to squeeze through the window.

"Don't turn this around on me! Father and the others think you should drop a few too, you chubby-"

Matthew slid through the window just in time to interrupt Jonathan's would-be insult, landing belly-first on the floor in the process. The big man didn't stay down long as he immediately sprung up to his feet with a look of sudden panic on his face.

"GHHHHHHHAAAAAAAA!!!" He cried out, while frantically brushing shards of tiny glass off himself.

"Toilet Flush! Are you ok?!" Jonathan asked, wincing as he stared at the shards.

"*heavy breathing* Yeah I'm good." A cocky smile formed on his face. "This Big'ol Belly of mine was perfectly equipped to withstand the impact."

"...Fuck you, I know that hurt like Sink Pisser Hell."

"Still does." He rubbed his stomach, masking his pain with a shit-eating grin. "But a big man like me can take the pain. A little man like you would still be crying on the floor."

"*sigh* Whatever, let's just grab this guy already."

"Lead the way, 'Little Man'."

Jonathan flicked the flashlight mounted to his beanbag gun on and began searching the living room. Matthew would soon join in after rubbing his belly for a bit longer. However, just as the big man began his search, he noticed Jonathan making his way out of the room.

"Hey! Where do you think you're going?"

"To the kitchen?" Jonathan bluntly replied. "I've already finished sweeping this room."

"Oh, uh, good job. I would have done it faster though, so step up your game!"

Jonathan stopped walking while rolling his eyes. "Sure, I'll get right on that. Actually, you know what, how about you assist me with 'stepping up my game' by, you know, **helping me?**"

"Well, I normally prefer my trainees-"

"Dude, shut the fuck up with this 'training' bullshit." Jonathan interrupted. "You and I both know you're barely higher than me in the pecking order."

"...So you admit I still outrank you?"

"*sigh* Fine, you 'outrank' me, happy? Can we start our sweep of the kitchen now?"

"Haha, yeah, I was already planning on doing that anyways. Just wanted to, uhh, make sure we had an *understanding.*"

"Alright. Great." Jonathan resumed his walk. "Let's just get going already."

Matthew couldn't think of another sly remark, so just followed him into the kitchen. Admittedly, he was impressed with Jonathan's willingness to take initiative in their search. Whether or not that was due to the consequences of pissing off The Father didn't matter at that moment, as Jonathan at the very least was showing his potential.

While thinking about this, he noticed Jonathan had come to a sudden stop after taking a few steps into the kitchen. Before Matthew could inquire about this, Jonathan turned to him with a disgusted look on his face.

"It smells like gross alcohol in here... Strong gross alcohol."

"Strong gross alcohol?" Matthew asked while stepping into the kitchen. "*sniff* *sniff* Wait a minute, is that? *sniff* *sniff* *sniff*"

Matthew shined his light around the kitchen, quickly spotting William's Pooer Brewer™. The big bounty hunter's eyes lit up with an almost man-child-like glee that Jonathan had never seen before.

"TOILET SHINE!!!"

Matthew rushed up to the Pooer Brewer™ in alcoholic joy, dropping his beanbag gun in the process. Jonathan was quick to grab the gun before it hit the ground. He immediately looked up to chastise Matthew for his recklessness, only to be met with the disturbing sight of the big man scooping handfuls of the liquid into his mouth.

"Wh-What the fuck are you doing?!"

Matthew didn't respond. The call of mixed alcohol was just too strong for him to ignore.

"Dammit you fat fuck, we need to focus on finding that Sink Pissing Bastard!"

He turned to face Jonathan with a euphoric look on his face. The alcoholic concoction had covered his mouth and leaked down to his vest.

"You've got this! If you need help, just yell and I'll come running!"

He went back to drinking with blissful purpose. The Toilet Shine splashed all over Matthew and dripped down on the floor. Jonathan gagged from the now-strengthened smell and gently placed Matthew's beanbag gun on the counter before stepping out of the kitchen.

"How in The Toilet's name do people enjoy that putrid shit?" He asked himself, getting grossed out at the thought of the concoction's popularity.

After recovering, he resumed his search for William. Figuring Matthew had the kitchen "secured", Jonathan shifted his attention to a nearby bedroom door. While approaching the door, he hesitated for a moment and questioned if it was smart to enter without Matthew backing him up. But soon came to his own justified realization that this was the perfect way to prove his worth to The Father.

"You've got this… You've fucking got this…"

Jonathan slowly opened the door at first, stopping momentarily as fear nearly overtook him. But after a quick personal pep talk, he would gain the courage to swing the door open and march in with his gun pointing forward. However, this sudden burst of confidence was lost almost immediately as he was met with the horrifying sight of William standing armed with a baseball bat within swinging distance.

Before the inexperienced bounty hunter could react, William attempted to strike. Jonathan instinctively blocked the bat with his gun. The impact of the strike caused him to fire the gun off towards the ceiling while dropping it to the ground. This startled both of them, causing William to stumble back and Jonathan to run away.

"Help! I need help!" Jonathan cried out while running into the kitchen.

"Wha- What?!" Matthew shot up, clearly buzzed. "What's going on?"

"I found him! He's armed with a bat in the-"

Jonathan, in his reckless panic, suddenly slipped on the Toilet Shine covered floor. He screamed for a split second before smacking the side of his head on the counter and landing lifelessly on the floor. It took a moment for Matthew to register the severity of watching his fellow bounty hunter in training take himself out, but it eventually clicked.

"...Uh-oh."

Matthew rushed up to his body with newfound urgency. After a quick inspection, he realized "The Little Man" was knocked unconscious.

"Oh fuck! Fuck fuck fuuuuuuck!!"

Matthew's panic would only be amplified as an old weather-beaten axe began smashing through the upper half of the front door. That fear would then reach its peak as The Father looked in through the now-destroyed door with a flashlight illuminating his enraged face.

"William has escaped through a window into the woods! How did you two allow this to happen?!"

Matthew stood frozen in fear. He couldn't work up the nerve to explain how badly his Toilet Shine addiction had ruined such a simple and important task.

"You better start explaining yourself!" The Father smashed through the remaining bit of the door and climbed in over a couch that was shoved against the door. **"And where's Jonathan!?"**

Matthew looked down at Jonathan's unconscious body, dreading how The Father would react to seeing him in such a state. Unable to bring himself to tell the truth, the big man quickly thought up a lie.

"W-William was prepared for us!" He dragged Jonathan's body into view. "That Sink Pissing bastard knocked poor little Jonathan out with a baseball bat!"

The Father entered the kitchen to get a better look at Jonathan. His attention though shifted once he gotta whiff of the Toilet Shine covering Matthew.

"You weren't drinking on the job... **Were you?**"

"No! I- I swear I wasn't! We approached William in the kitchen, and he splashed a bunch of Toilet Shine in my eyes! When I regained my sight, Jonathan was lying unconscious on the floor!"

The Father stared at Matthew for a good five seconds, seemingly debating on whether or not he believed him. "So, you believe that he was prepared for us? Or at the very least, knew 'someone' might 'take things into their own hands', and come for him?"

"Y- Yes! That's the only way he could have easily gotten the jump on us."

The Father again stared for a moment, before clenching his fist. "One of those damn Toilet-Quisitors probably gave him the heads up! Those bastards have always been interfering in my jobs..."

Matthew breathed an internal sigh of relief. "So, what's our next course of action?"

"What do you mean? We're going to track that Sink Pissing bastard down." The Father replied, talking down to Matthew as if he were a fool.

"But…" Matthew looked down at Jonathan. "What about Jonathan? We can't just leave him here like this."

"We'll call an ambulance. In the meantime, my daughter can look after him." The Father grabbed the beanbag gun off the counter and handed it to Matthew. "Now, let's go catch that worthless Sink Pisser."

Matthew happily took his gun, ready for action. Before they left though, one last question remained.

"But, sir, how will we track that Sink Pisser down? He could be anywhere in the woods by now."

"Matthew, you're talking to a man with 30 years of bounty hunter experience." He placed his hand on Matthew's shoulder. "I have successfully tracked exactly 72 people in the woods. Do you think I'd just let William rush out there if I didn't think we'd be able to hunt him down?"

Despite The Father's seemingly calm tone, Matthew could sense of hint of rage over being questioned. He knew it was best just to go along with it.

"No Sir, I have complete faith in you..."

"Good... Now let's go catch that worthless Sink Pisser."

Le Fifth Chapter

A Sink Pissing Sinner's Remorse

Distraught... Scared... Betrayed... and yet still so ashamed... All of these hostile thoughts stabbed at William's emotionally shattered mind.

However, it wasn't the shame of being a no-good Sink Pisser that devastated him. At least, not entirely. No, what truly sapped William's soul away was his undeniably selfish betrayal of his loving wife.

For years the two had worked so hard to build their wonderful little life together. From the harsh backbreaking physical labor of William's lumberjack job, to his wife's proud yet tedious religious career as a plumber, their hard work had paid off in the form of a perfect house for two... And soon to be three. Such tightly bound love, no matter the ups and downs that came with it, was thought to be unbreakable.

But William, despite his foolish act of blasphemy, was smart enough to know he had, quite literally, pissed it all away.

That tainting moment, when she witnessed him in the act played on repeat in William's head. He would have given anything to go back in time and stop himself from giving into his sinfully shortsighted decision to go against their faith and ruin what could have been a perfect toilet-loving family.

…But there was no going back. Even if his wife was willing to forgive him, too many people already wanted "justice" carried out. William's fate was set in stone, and he had no one else to blame but himself.

So now, William's only course of action left was to sit alone, hidden away in the temporary safety of his job's warehouse. Where he would helplessly await for either The Father or Toilet-Quisitor to track him down and bring his life to an end…

Except, this Sink Pisser wasn't about to just lay down and die so easily.

Some might say it was just a man's natural survival instinct, while others would claim desperation was at play. However, the true reason William refused to lay his life down so willingly was much more personal.

His legacy and reputation were already down the shitter, and nothing would ever change that. However, if William was already a dead man walking, then at the very least he'd want the world to remember him as a man who went down fighting.

...For, in the end, that was the closest thing to a victory William would get in this unwinnable battle *for his life*.

Of Lumber
And Retribution

After about ten or so minutes of expertly tracking William's footsteps deeper and deeper into the woods, The Father had led his men to an old sawmill. While his men couldn't figure out why "That Sink Pisser" would retreat to such a seemingly random location, it all made sense to The Father.

"I'm familiar with this place." He began while carefully examining the various buildings and large lumber equipment spread around the area. "He could be hiding out anywhere in here, so we-"

"But, Sir?" Tyler interrupted. "How do ya know William is-"

The Father backhanded him, causing him to stumble a few steps back. **"Let me finish!"**

Tyler attempted to enter a Soldier Stance while rubbing his now slightly crooked nose. "S-Sorry Sir!"

The Father stared him down momentarily, before turning to face the lumber yard. "To answer your question, my daughter mentioned this is where William worked, and I've seen so many of my past targets retreat to their places of employment for safety. I do not know why this is so common, but that's just how it is for whatever reason."

He turned back to his men, looking directly at Tyler. "Now as I was saying. We must split up, and-"

The Father's cell phone went off, causing him to tense up with rage. As he pulled it out, his men were sure it would snap in two with how tightly he was gripping it. To their surprise, The Father would loosen his grip once he realized who was calling.

"What is it, darling?" He semi-casually answered.

A voice, which the men knew belonged to his daughter, was heard explaining something. While they couldn't make out what she was saying, they could tell it was something serious by how shocked The Father looked.

"What?! So you mean to tell me..."

He stopped himself, looking over to his men.

"I want you three to search the lumber mill! I have-" He looked directly at Matthew before finishing. "**Important** matters to discuss with my daughter."

Matthew's blood ran cold. Or, alcoholic blood, in this case, as the past ten minutes were more than enough time for all that Toilet Shine he consumed to leave him fully drunk.

"Uhh, umm, y- ya- yes Sh- Sir!" Matthew saluted, trying to hide his slurred speech.

"...Good." He walked past the three, going back towards the way they came. "I'll return shortly. In the meantime, I'm leaving Noah temporarily in charge."

"Wait, you're letting me be in charge?" Noah beamed.

"Temporarily!" The Father emphasized. "Don't fuck this up!"

The three watched The Father walk off before Matthew and Tyler turned to Noah for further instructions. It didn't take long for him to calm his excitement and soon was ready to lead.

"Alright men, here's the plan." He began while turning towards the warehouse. "You two investigate the warehouse, as it's more than likely he'd try to hide out in the largest building."

He then turned towards a smaller building close to the warehouse. "I'll do a quick sweep of, what I assume is the main saw building, then join back up with you two in the warehouse."

He finally turned back to them. "Do I make myself…"

While Tyler was obviously paying attention, Matthew looked to be zoning out while staring blankly at a random tree stump.

"Matthew!" Noah yelled, getting up in his face. "Wha? Ohh uhh-" Matthew spluttered while entering a Soldier Stance. "What Shir?! I mean, yes Sir! Where do you **hiccup** need me?"

Noah clenched his fist, fighting the urge to sock him in the face. "What in the Sink Pissing Hell is going on with you?!"

"N-Nothing! I'm perfectly- **beeeeelch**"

Noah narrowed his eyes, as the disgustingly familiar smell of Toilet Dew entered his nostrils. "You fucking lied to The Father about drinking on the job, didn't you…"

"W-Well-"

"Don't fucking deny it!"

Matthew knew there was no reason, **or way**, to hide it anymore. "I did, ok? I- I just couldn't resist! It had been so long since I had any!"

Noah stepped away from the two, turning his back to them while staring at the ground. "Just… Just go in there with Tyler and search for that Sink Pissing bastard. Hopefully, if we manage to find him, that **might** be enough to calm The Father down when he discovers the truth… If he hasn't already, that is."

"**gulp** D-Don't worry, I won't let-"

"You've already let me, **and the rest of us**, down." Noah chastised while beginning to make his way toward the saw building. "Tyler, make sure this fuck up doesn't fuck up anymore."

These harsh yet accurate words sliced deep into Matthew's pride. He was used to Noah making fun of his weight, or even the occasional remarks directed toward his love of drinking on the job. But this… This was pure hatred mixed with soul-crushing disappointment.

It was enough to make him cry. Or it would have been if Tyler didn't smack him upside the head.

"Yall heard Noah! Let's go find ourselves a Sink Pisser! Otherwise, it'll be your fat piggy ass!"

"I know." Matthew sniffled. "Lead the way…"

Tyler made his way up to the warehouse. Matthew followed behind, staggering a bit but managing to keep up without issue… Unfortunately, he would lose his balance right as they made it up to the old wooden enterence doors, and smashed right through them.

"Got dang it Matt! Ya fat fucking fuck!" He kicked him in the side of his abdomen. "If that Sink Pisser didn't already know we were here, then he does now!"

"But…" Matthew began while getting back up. "We're not even sure if he's in here or not. For all we know-"

Tyler kicked him again, knocking him back to the ground. "Point still stands! You shouldn't be making so much got dang noise! You big belly bastard!"

"Okay okay, I get it!"

"I hope so. Now, get your fat ass up and start-"

The lights in the warehouse all at once suddenly came on. The two were momentarily thrown into a blind panic, frantically looking around as their eyes adjusted.

"Got dammit!" Tyler yelled out while pointing his gun every which way. "Get ready! That bastard is gonna jump us!"

"I-I'm ready for him! This Sink Pisser doesn't know who he's dealing…" As Matthew shot up to his feet, he was met with the blurry sight of The Father gripping the switch of a mounted metal power box.

"What is it?!" Tyler yelled, pointing his gun in the direction Matthew was staring. "Do you see-"

"Do NOT aim your gun at me!" The Father ordered while pointing his axe at Tyler.

"F-Father!?" Tyler shuddered, nearly dropping his gun. "I-I Didn't mean to make ya mad! P-P-Please forgive me, Sir!"

The Father lowered his axe and removed his hand from the switch. "I'm not mad at you, I just don't feel like being shot."

"Haha, yeah those things hurt like Sink Pisser Hell" Matthew chuckled. "I still remember when Noah shot me in the ass that one-"

"But I'm FUCKING LIVID with you, Matthew!" The Father exploded, shaking with rage.

"Wh-Why?!" Matthew panicked, instinctively backing away from The Father. "Di-Did I do somethin wrong?!"

"You lied to me!" The Father accused while marching towards him. "My daughter found Jonathan's rifle lying damaged in the bedroom! AND noticed a gunshot hole in the ceiling! Prey tell me how this is possible if, based on what YOU told me, the two of you were jumped in the kitchen!?"

"Uhhh, well, *hiccup* umm-"

The Father shoved him against a bundle of wood. "You're a fool, but you can't play dumb with me!" He slammed the head of his axe into the wood, missing Matthew by only an inch. "You got drunk off that wretched alcohol concoction and left Jonathan to fend for himself!!"

Matthew could feel his heart thumping harder than ever before in his life. He had seen this sort of rage from The Father many times in the past, and it always ended with a dead target. Now, he feared the wrong choice of words may end with him suffering the same fate.

"W-Well, ya- you s-sh-see, Jonathan went after that Sink Pisser by himself t-to prove-"

"Don't fucking lie to me!" The Father ripped the axe out of the wood and shoved the handle against his neck. **"Are you prepared to die over this?!"**

"Dammit man, just tell the truth already." Tyler huffed, looking down at the ground. "There's no reason to hide it now."

Feeling the life practically be choked out of him, Matthew's eyes darted all around for any potential way of escape. Even if the next words he spat out were the truth, his panicked and drunken mind couldn't foresee things ending well.

However, in his desperate search, he caught a glimpse of William approaching Tyler while armed with a bat. He was only a few feet away and looked ready to knock his partner out.

"I-It- *choking* I-"

"What?!" The Father let up. "Out with it!"

Matthew took a few seconds to catch his breath, before pointing behind Tyler. "Look out! It's *quick heavy breath* The Sink Pisser!"

William froze up like a deer in headlights as all eyes were now set on him. Tyler similarly froze up, not even thinking to point his gun at the Sink Pissing criminal standing right in front of him. This lack of action was something The Father wouldn't stand for.

"What are you doing!? Shoot that bastard already!"

Neither Tyler nor William appeared to be paying any attention to The Father. Instead, they were caught in what could only be described as a stunned deadlock with each other, both too scared to make the first move.

The Father, as expected, was not at all pleased. Such a pathetic sight normally would have thrown The Father into a rage. However, given how exceptionally bad their mission had been going up to that point, he could only bring himself to be disappointed.

Matthew took notice of how unusually soul-crushed The Father was and realized it was time for him to redeem himself… Well, more so time to save his own ass from whatever "retribution" he should have suffered, but redemption sounded a lot nicer.

"Don't worry- **burp** Sir! I've gh- got this!" Matthew recklessly fired his gun without aiming. His shot completely missed William and instead nailed Tyler right in his neck.

"...Oh shit."

A painfully loud and wet snapping sound echoed out as Tyler's neck bent at an unnatural angle. He coughed up some blood as he collapsed, twitching violently once making impact with the ground. William, not wanting to suffer a similar fate, took off into the maze of wooden bundles. Just in time too, as The Father rushed up to inspect Tyler only a few seconds later.

"T-Tyler! Are you…"

He didn't bother finishing, as Tyler's body had stopped moving the moment he kneeled. The poor guy was too far gone to be saved.

"You killed him…" The Father got to his feet, setting his hateful gaze on Matthew. "You fucking killed him..."

"I-I-I- *hiccup* I-"

"BY TOILET, BE PURGED!!!" The Father roared like a warlord, charging forward with his axe raised high in the air.

"AHHHHH!!!!" Matthew cried out at the top of his lungs while lunging forward. **"I AIN'T READY TO DIE!!!"**

Using every bit of drunken Toilet Shine-empowered strength he could muster, Matthew smashed the butt-stock of his gun right between The Father's eyes.

Time felt as if it had slowed down for Matthew as he watched his skull-cracking strike knock The Father off his feet. Blood had quickly begun to leak from his forehead, spraying a bit throughout the air. Shards from his now shattered glasses scattered all around, with a few having been embedded into his brow.

It was only when the back of The Father's head slammed against the floor did Matthew's short-lived burst of adrenaline wear off, and the reality of what he had done kicked in.

"Oh… Oh no…"

Staring down at his, now-former, teacher, The Father stared back at him… But there was no sign of life in his cold eyes. One of the greatest Big Toilet Bounty Hunters to have ever lived, now laid dead and broken in front of his student. Matthew wouldn't have long to think on this though, as-

"What have you done?!" Noah exploded, watching on from the entrance.

"Whhaahhha!!!" Matthew squealed, nearly scared sober. "W-Wait! I- *hiccup* I- I didn't mean to do it!!"

"Didn't mean to do it?!?!"

Noah fired at Matthew, snapping his right knee with a well-placed bean bag.

"GHHHHHAAAAAAHHHH!!!!" He cried out, collapsing to the floor while gripping his devastated knee.

"Oops, I didn't mean to do that!" Noah belittled while making his way toward The Father's body. "But I'm sure The Father will understand… Oh wait, **he's fucking dead!!!**"

Matthew pushed himself up a little with his hands, staring at Noah with an exaggeratedly pitiful look on his face. "**sobs** P-Please Noah, I really didn't mean to- **sobs** kill Tyler and-"

"Shut it!" Noah snapped, spear-throwing his gun at him.

He completely missed, breaking his gun in the process. Despite this, he was still successful in "shutting him up".

"I knew you'd be trouble the moment your fat ass join our group! If I had my way back then, you… Wait, Tyler?" Noah looked around, soon spotting Tyler's body. "You… You worthless piece of outhouse shit…"

Matthew cried harder than ever before in his life. "I- I swear on- *sobs* Toilet that it was an accident!"

"Accident!? **Accident!?!?**" Noah ripped the axe from The Father's cold dead hands. "I'll show you an **accident!!!**"

He marched up to the drunken sobbing mess of a man, staring at him as if he were just another target. Matthew could only watch on helplessly while lying broken on the ground. He knew it was the end of the line, but just couldn't fully accept it.

"Please, Noah! *sobs* Don't do this!!!"

He looked down at Matthew for a good few seconds, then lifted the axe high into the air. "It's time for **you** to suffer an 'axe-ident'!"

"Noooooo!!! NOOOOOOOOO-"

Noah brought the axe down on his head with the force of an industrial septic tank, bringing a swift end to Matthew. With him dead, the vengeful rage that had overtaken Noah vanished... Only for a disgusting realization to soak in.

"O-Oh- *gags*"

To spare you the gory details, Noah was covered head to toe in Matthew's "Chunky Head Sauce".

"**gags** Oh Toilet, I- **gags** think I'm gonna- **gags**"

Noah rushed out of the warehouse, vomiting the moment he made it outside. The burning pain of his stomach being emptied caused him to start thinking about his job on a much deeper level than usual.

He had always known, or at least figured, that he'd have to be the one to take someone's life at some point. Not everyone could be brought in alive after all, and The Father wouldn't be around forever to do the deadly deed. However, nothing could have prepared him for how disgustingly violent it would end up being. **Especially** when done in such an overly brutal way.

This thought would suddenly be put on hold though, as loud stomps could be heard fast approaching him from behind. At that moment, the reason he and his now-dead team were there would return to Noah.

"Sink Pisser!" He yelled out while turning around, axe ready to use. "**Stand down, or I wi-** **gasp**!"

WHACK

Noah had only gotten a split-second view of William's bat before it smacked against his nose and knocked him on his back. The dark star-filled sky was the last thing Noah saw, before blacking out on the ground.

William watched the man for a moment, ready to swing again if needed. Soon though, he would realize the first strike was effective… Perhaps a bit too effective, as Noah was no longer breathing.

"Dammit, y-you just had to turn around didn't you?!" William huffed, lowering his bat. "I- I didn't want to kill you…"

"But you did, Mr. Wangle." The distressfully familiar voice of an older-sounding man chimed in from a distance.

William snapped his head up, eyes darting around in every direction. "Wh- Who are you!? Show yourself!"

"Oh come now, Mr. Wangle." The man answered, walking into the dim outdoor light of the warehouse for William to see. "We spoke on the phone earlier. Have you already forgotten?"

From his bright red robes to his pure golden toilet seat necklace that shined so brightly in the dim light, William's blood ran cold as he laid his eyes on the religiously dressed old man. It only took a few seconds for him to realize the danger he was in.

"You're… You're that ***Toilet-Quisitor…***"

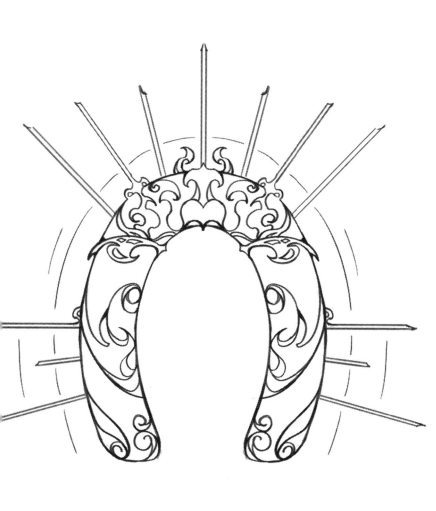

Le Seventh Chapter

Death's Justice Courtesy Of The Toilet-Quisitor

Frozen with fear and clenching his bat with a stone-tight grip, William could only watch as the Toilet-Quisitor stared him down. It felt as if Death himself was sizing him up for the perfect one-way trip to Sink Pisser Hell. Even The Father could never awaken such a primordial sense of dread.

Their "stare down", if you could even call it that, suddenly ended as The Toilet-Quisitor's eyes would lay themselves upon Noah's dead body. He didn't seem to care for the young man's death. If anything, the mildly annoyed look on his face was comparable to that of a boss spotting some trash on the floor.

"You've been quite busy, Mr. Wangle." The Toilet-Quisitor stated, keeping his eyes fixed on Noah. "Is it safe to assume you murdered the others as well? If so, where would I find their bodies?"

William felt almost offended by his assumption. "I- I didn't kill anyone else. They killed each other in the warehouse."

"Right…"

The Toilet-Quisitor began making his way forward, causing William to raise his bat in defense.

Before he could work up the nerve to strike or even say anything, The Toilet-Quisitor kneeled to inspect Noah's body.

"Mr. Wangle, while I may not have liked The Father all that much, to suggest that someone like him would be killed by incompetence is quite hard to believe... However, all this bloodshed you've caused means little to me. What's important is that, along with your sinful act, you are now also guilty of mass murder, and nothing will change that."

William so desperately wanted to bring his bat down on The Toilet-Quisitor, but the direct accusation of guilt pissed him off. So much so that he, quite foolishly, let his guard down.

"M-Mass murder?! I'm not gonna take the blame for-"

The Toilet-Quisitor sprung forward in the blink of an eye, socking him in the gut with righteous religious fury that only an aged champion of faith could deliver. William clenched his stomach as the wind was knocked out of him. He nearly collapsed forward onto the ground, only stopping his fall at the last moment by planting his knees and bat-clenching fist into the ground.

"I don't think you understand, Mr. Wangle." The Toilet-Quisitor began, looking down on William with a vicious gaze that didn't match his calm tone. "Or shall I refer to you as… Sink Pisser?"

William lacked the will, and more importantly, the oxygen to reply. All he could do was listen on while trying to catch his breath.

"Listen to me, 'Sink Pisser Wangle', I will be upfront with you." The Toilet-Quisitor stepped back about 6 feet, presumably to give each other some space. "I have never failed to bring a Sink Pisser to justice, and every attempt at resisting me has only led to a *swift, brutal, yet still non-lethal beating* of those foolish enough to try… So, I will only ask this once. Are you willing to peacefully come with me, or shall I 'make a *'pale-faced fool'* out of you?"

William, after taking in enough air to sorta recover, slowly got to his feet. "I… I might be a short-sighted fool who didn't think things through…"

The Toilet-Quisitor simply gave nothing more than a pridefully smug smile in response. However, he would only get to take one step towards William, before William took one of his own.

"But I will NOT go down like a turd in a toilet!"

He charged forward with clear violent intent, wiping away The Toilet-Quisitor's smile as quickly as it came. The trouble and bullshit that had been thrown William's way that night had filled "The Sink Pisser" with a level of barbaric fury he had never experienced. All of which was used to fuel a mighty swing of his bat strong enough to deliver a decisive killing blow.

Unfortunately for William…

"You've made your choice, Mr. Wangle."

The Toilet-Quisitor sidestepped out of the way, causing William to throw himself past by a couple of feet. With the two's backs now facing each other, The Toilet-Quisitor swung his right elbow up in the air while gripping his right fist with his left hand.

"Now, it is time for you to suffer the same fate as those other fools."

Bringing down the ballistic wrath of both arms, The Toilet-Quisitor slammed his right elbow into the lower back of William.

"GHHHHHHHHAAAAAAAAAHHHHHH!!!!"

A booming crackle echoed out as a puncturing wave of pain shot through William's entire body. It felt as if the horn of a bull had pierced his spine, and tore into his nerves with the surgical precision of a heartless surgeon.

Such an overwhelming shock to William's system caused him to collapse. The damage didn't end there though, as his chin smacked against a rock embedded in the ground. He could feel his teeth cracking and jaw dislocating in agonizing synergy. This alone would have been enough to destroy any man's will to live, but paired with the nerves in his back crying to be put out of their misery, one can only shutter while trying to imagine the torment William was forced to endure.

His face had turned pale as a corpse, with his body twitching as if he were suffering from a seizure. To the untrained eye, it would have appeared that

William was in the process of dying… To The Toilet-Quisitor though, this was nothing more than a *swift, brutal, yet still non-lethal beating.*

"Congratulations, Sink Pisser Wangle, you are yet another *pale-faced fool* to fall before me." The Toilet-Quisitor mocked while turning around to look down at William. "Any last words, before I, as the younglings would say, 'knock your Toiletroom lights out'?"

William, quite predictably, was unable to speak. Hell, he likely didn't register a single thing being said to him.

"Nothing? Well then…" The Toilet-Quisitor casually walked up next to William's head, lining himself up for the perfect kick. "You're just like the *others.*"

As The Toilet-Quisitor brought his leg back, William summoned just enough strength to turn his head in an attempt to see what was happening… Only to catch the last few seconds of a heavily used steal toe boot coming down towards him, before everything went black.

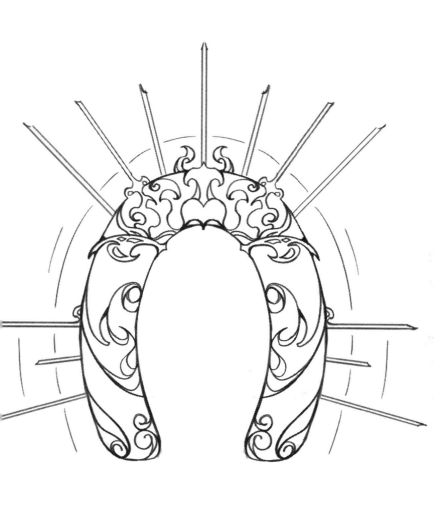

Le Eighth Chapter

The End OF William Wangle

As William slowly regained consciousness, so too did his senses return. All at once, an unforgiving wave of aches and pains shot through his back, jaw, and head from the beating he had been on the receiving end of. The poor guy didn't even get the courtesy of rubbing his broken face, as his arms had been tied behind his back. This, however, was pushed far to the side as the distressfully familiar voices of an enraged crowd were heard chanting an oh-so-familiar insult.

"Sink Pisser!!!!"

        "Sink Pisser!!!!"

            "Sink Pisser!!!!"

        "Sink Pisser!!!!"

"Sink Pisser!!!!"

        "Sink Pisser!!!!"

            "Sink Pisser!!!!"

        "Sink Pisser!!!!"

"Sink Pisser!!!!"

        "Sink Pisser!!!!"

            "Sink Pisser!!!!"

Snapping his eyes open and confirming a bloodthirsty crowd of his fellow town's folk were ready to kill him, William realized his world had been turned upside down... Literally, as he was hanging upside down above a large toilet-shaped gallow, by a rope tightly tied around his ankles.

"The great Toilets above gifted you a penis, and you foolishly chose to use it by **PISSING IN A SINK!!!**" A random teenage guy raged.

"Yeah! I might just come up there and chop that troublesome willy off!" A wheelchair-bound old lady added.

"TOILET!!!" A religious Toilet fanatic man roared, suddenly charging the gallow.

The fanatic pushed and shoved through the crowd, knocking anyone in his way to the ground. While most of the people simply cleared a way for the justifiably unhinged man, a few found his unrelenting devotion inspiring.

"This guy has the right idea!" A middle-aged man began praising. "That good-for-nothing Sink Pisser deserves way worse than some basic corporate execution!"

He and five other people joined in on rushing the gallow. This included the old lady, who's wheel chair was being pushed by the enraged teenager.

William, anticipating a fate worse than death as he knew from past executions that the old lady always followed through with her threats, prayed that the Toilet Gods would take pity and allow for the fanatic to kill him first. It would, at the very least, be a quicker and **significantly** less painful death than what she had planned.

However, just as the fanatic took his first step on the gallows stairs, an earsplitting gunshot rang out. The crowd went silent and watched as a bullet flew straight through the fanatics' chest. Once his lifeless body hit the ground, everyone looked over to the source of the shot.

To their, well, sorta but not really surprise, they saw The Toilet-Quisitor with a Church-built pistol in his hand. Next to him stood a woman dressed in business attire. While none of them knew who she was, her exceptionally fake smile gave away that she worked for Big Toilet™. They wouldn't have long to think on this though, as The Toilet-Quisitor fired a shot into the air.

"*I will not allow another execution to be ruined by a lack of patience!*" He pointed his gun at the others who followed the fanatic. "*Do I make myself clear?*"

They fearfully nodded, quickly integrating back into the crowd.

"*Good...*" He holstered his gun. "Come along Sheryl, let's get this over with before someone else rushes the gallow."

"That would be very unfortunate, as you would have to shoot another person." She replied, with no emotion in her voice whatsoever.

"...I'm shocked you didn't say 'customer'."

"You mean, 'custo-more'? Ha. Ha. Ha." She joked, her tone not once changing, even while laughing.

"*sigh* Whatever."

With order now restored, for the moment at least, The Toilet-Quisitor and Sheryl made their way up the gallow. Once reaching the top, William stared at them in, well to be blunt, pants-shitting terror… Minus the pants-shitting part, thankfully.

Despite having attended quite a few Sink Pisser executions, William had never gotten a chance to see an actual execution take place. Enraged fanatics, and a certain old lady, had always killed or brutalized the heretics before local government officials could subject them to their fates.

Horrific thoughts of terrible execution methods soon pulled William into the darkest corners of his mind. He began to wonder if being murdered by The Father would have been a much better way to go out, or if simply surrendering to The Toilet-Quisitor when offered would have resulted in a significantly more lenient execution.

His mind then shifted to the Big Toilet™ employee. For all he knew, she was there to provide top-secret Big Toilet™ methods of execution. Or even worse, an unholy combination of religious and corporate executions that bordered on torture.

Before the endless pit that was his paranoia could pull William down further, Sheryl smacked him across the face, intentionally avoiding his devastated jaw.

"Please be smart and stay focused, William." She advised while kneeling down to stare at him with her soulless corporate eyes. "I was informed by my boss, who was informed by his boss, who was informed by his boss, that I might receive a promotion if this execution remained family-friendly."

No amount of words could accurately describe the complete 180 William's mind took at that moment.

"F... Family-friendly?"

"Yes, family-friendly." She confirmed. "Now, in the end, it isn't up to me how violently that Toilet-Quisitor kills you. However, I have convinced him to go with the least bloody form of execution. So please refrain from ANYTHING that might even remotely make him angry."

William was now more confused than ever. "But... But... Why would-"

"**gasp** He's about to start his speech!" She interrupted while springing to her feet. "Now, be a good Sink Pisser, stay quiet, and stay focused."

Sheryl rushed to The Toilet-Quisitor's side. Just in time too, as he began giving his speech.

"*People of Grand Bowl!!!*" He began, while raising his arms into the air. "*We gather here tonight to end the life of this worthless Sink Pisser!!!*"

The crowd let out a booming round of applause, with a few people beginning to chant **"TOILET"** at the top of their lungs.

"*However!*" The Toilet-Quisitor interrupted, once again silencing the crowd. "*I can NOT in good conscience be the one to perform the execution... Given that your local Bounty Hunting Champion of Big Toilet™ was slain while trying to capture this Sink Pissing Piece Of Shit!*"

The crowd gasped, shifting their hateful collective gaze upon William.

"N-No!" William cried out in defense. "I wasn't the one who- *jaw cracks*"

It was no use. Wiliam's devastated jaw gave out before he could finish. All he could do was hang there and take the crowd's vengeful rage.

"Y-Y-You fucking monster!" The town's doctor fumed.

"I can't believe I used to subtly flirt with you while ringing up your groceries!" A woman in her young 20s fumed, sounding more heartbroken than anything else.

Some old dude tried to yell something, but his overwhelming rage caused him to suffer a heart attack and immediately die.

"*gasp* Oh my Toilet!!!" A middle-aged woman standing next to the now-dead old man cried out. **"That Sink Pisser took another life!!!"**

Everyone looked ready to unleash their own personal inner beasts of toilet rage. Before any of them could act on these berserked impulses, some woman charged up with a rock in her hand… Except, this wasn't just "some woman".

"*You're the worst thing that ever happened to this town!!!*" Vanessa, William's now ex-wife and, potentially more importantly, The Father's daughter, denounced.

William braced himself for the rock-hard impact. However, just as she was about to cast her stone, The Toilet-Quisitor shot it out of her hand.

"*Do NOT interfere!*" He roared, while keeping his gun pointed at her. "*You're lucky I take pity on you, given your circumstances. However, my mercy only goes so far, and I will not hesitate to kill you where you stand if you try anything else!*"

Vanessa, now shaking with fear, stepped back while nodding her head.

"*Good...*" He holstered his gun. "*Now...* Wait, where was I?"

Sheryl leaned in close to him. "You can't in good conscience be the one to perform the execution."

"Oh right."

He again rose his arms into the air.

"*In order to properly honor the legacy of such an exceptionally skilled Bounty Hunter, I have allowed for this Sink Pisser to be executed by one of Big Toilet's™ corporate employees!*" The Toilet-Quisitor lowered his arms, directing everyone's attention to Sheryl. "*Without further ado, I leave his death in the hands of Sheryl!*"

The crowd gave her a glowing round of applause while The Toilet-Quisitor took up a position near two levers off to the side. With the limelight now shining on Sheryl, she happily waved and pulled a piece of paper from her pocket.

"This speech was written on Big Toilet™ brand paper! Which can be bought from-"

"Sheryl…" The Toilet-Quisitor interrupted. "I thought we agreed on no advertisements…"

"Sorry, natural habit."

After taking a moment to clear her throat, she began to give a speech of her own.

"Hello, people of Grand Bowl! Today, we are here to bring a Sink Pisser to justice! Not just for his betrayal to all Toilet Kind, but also for the murder of our legendary Bounty Hunter… And the murder of three trainees, and attempted murder of one."

The Toilet-Quisitor pulled one of the levers, causing a portion of the wooden panels under William to slowly open. Once fully opened, deep water was revealed to have been stored underneath the floor.

W-Water? William questioned to himself. What are they planning on doing with…

The realization finally hit him, and the giant Toilet-shaped gallow soon made complete sense. He wouldn't have long to think on this though, as he noticed Sheryl had pulled out a pistol of her own.

"I can personally think of no better way to honor such a wonderful man than to kill his murderer using the Big Toilet™ approved method

of execution." She shot the rope holding William up, dropping him head-first into the cold water. **"The Grand Flush™!"**

The Toilet-Quisitor pulled the second lever, and William soon found himself at the mercy of a powerful whirlpool. Despite every attempt at thrashing and struggling his way out, the ropes around his wrists and ankles just wouldn't allow for it. Nothing could save him from being sucked down through a man-sized pipe like a giant turd in a toilet.

After tumbling through the pipe, William ended up at ground level in a clear water-filled glass dome. The crowd quickly gathered around to watch him drown. While it was impossible to hear them, William could see their enthusiastic cheers and heartless laughs. However, one person in particular stood out to William the most. Watching on in unmoving silence was his wife.

Despite everything that had happened and all the clear anger she had thrown William's way after the Sink Pissing incident, he saw no hatred in her eyes. Instead, all he could see was a conflicting gaze of pure disappointment and unmistakable regret…

This would be the last thing William ever saw before everything once again went black…

THIS TIME

FOR GOOD

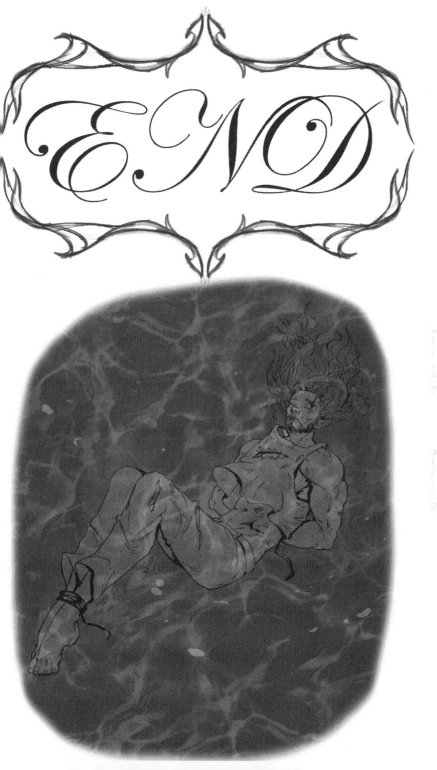

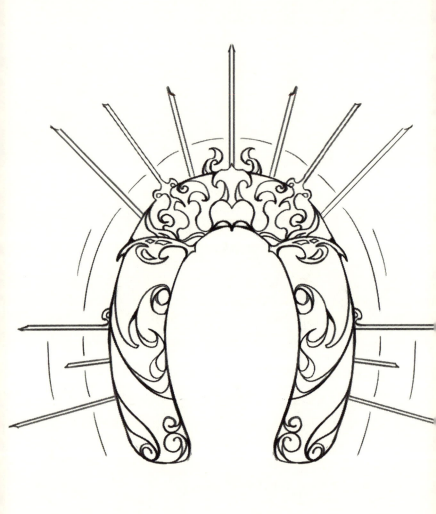

Made in the USA
Middletown, DE
20 August 2025